9 Deadly Self-Sabotage Behaviors

An Insight Into How To Overcome Self-Sabotaging Behaviors

Sensei Paul David

Copyright Page

9 Deadly Self-Sabotage Behaviors: An Insight Into How To Overcome Self-Sabotaging Behaviors, by Sensei Paul David

Copyright © 2022

All rights reserved.

978-1-77848-084-3 9 Deadly Self Sabotage Behaviors_Ingram_PaperbackBook

978-1-77848-083-6 9 Deadly Self Sabotage Behaviors_Amazon_PaperbackBook

978-1-77848-082-9 9 Deadly Self Sabotage Behaviors_Amazon_eBook

This book is not authorized for free distribution copying.

www.senseipublishing.com

@senseipublishing
#senseipublishing

Get/Share Our FREE All-Ages Mental Health Book Now!

FREE Self-Development Book for Every Family

senseiselfdevelopment.senseipublishing.com

Click Below or Search Amazon for Another Book In This Series

senseiselfdevelopment.senseipublishing.com

Join Our Publishing Journey!

If you would like to receive FUTURE FREE BOOKS and get to know us better, please click www.senseipublishing.com and join our newsletter by entering your email address in the pop-up box.

Follow Our Blog: senseipauldavid.ca

Follow/Like/Subscribe: Facebook, Instagram, YouTube: @senseipublishing

Scan the QR Code with your phone or tablet
to follow us on social media: Like / Subscribe / Follow

Thank You from The Author: Sensei Paul David

Before we dive in, I would like to thank you for picking up this book from among the many other similar books out there. Thank you for choosing to invest in my book. That means everything to me.

Now that you are here, I ask you to stick with me as we take your self-discovery journey together. I promise to make our time together valuable and worthwhile.

In the pages ahead, you will find some areas of information and practices more helpful than others - and that is great! I encourage you to apply what works best for you. You will benefit from the knowledge that you gain and the ensuing exciting transformation of character.

Enjoy!

Table of Contents

Introduction 1
Chapter One: Destroying Bridges 3
   Use Things, Love People 4
   Keeping Your Bridges Intact 7
Chapter Two: Self-Criticism 12
   You Are Not That Bad 13
   How To Overcome Self-Criticism 14
Chapter Three: Resistance To Change 21
   Changes Are Uncomfortable 21
   Change Is Necessary 23
   Dangers Of Resistance To Change 24
Chapter Four: Self-Neglect 29
   Causes of Self-Neglect 29
   How To Overcome Self-Neglect 34
Chapter Five: Procrastination 38
   Why Do People Procrastinate? 39
   How To Overcome Procrastination 42
Chapter Six: Perfectionism 46
   Signs Of Perfectionism 47
   How To Overcome Perfectionism 51

Chapter Seven: Impatience **55**
   Symptoms Of Impatience 55
   How To Overcome Impatience 59
Chapter Eight: Self-Objectification **65**
   You Are More Than Your Job 65
   Avoid The Temptation 68
   How To Overcome Self-Objectification 69
Chapter Nine: Distrust **73**
   The Dangers Of Extreme Lack Of Trust 73
   Why People Struggle To Trust Others 76
   How To Defeat Distrust 78
Conclusion **82**
References **84**

Foreword

Many people complain about individuals that act maliciously against them to prevent them from achieving the success they desire. Meanwhile, no one can stop you from attaining success unless you give up. The truth is that people can only delay your success or deny you certain opportunities. However, ultimately, you can achieve whatever you desire if you refuse to give up and of course, avoid shooting yourself in the foot.

In *9 Deadly Self-Sabotaging Behaviors*, Paul effectively combined research and anecdotal evidence to help us understand that success is not as elusive as we think. He points out nine acts of many people that make them live a miserable life full of regret. This masterpiece is a must-read for anyone trying to find the right formula for success and happiness.

Introduction

"What is required for many of us, paradoxical though it may sound, is the courage to tolerate happiness without self-sabotage."

Nathaniel Branden

I have wanted to start writing this book for the past six days but I did not start until today. Is it because of procrastination? Well, partially. However, what has been my major concern is how to write a book on self-sabotaging behaviors that will include nine of the deadliest of them all. The truth is that there are more than nine self-sabotaging behaviors.

Yet, a critical and meticulous study has helped me to understand that most of them can be classified under nine broad categories. My intention for writing yet another self-help book is the desire to help my readers have a better understanding of how to live a life where they feel empowered to live a successful life free of self-sabotage. This is my gift to you. I hope you enjoy it.

Chapter One: Destroying Bridges

Sadly, many people are their own worst enemies without realizing it. There are so many examples of prodigiously talented people who never fulfilled their potential because they shot themselves in the foot at some point. For the sake of respecting the journey and struggles of some people, I will not mention their names. Yet, every sphere of life has many stories of what could have been. This chapter will focus on how many people burn the bridges that could have led to their success, by disrespecting people they should have treated well.

Use Things, Love People

In the closing chapter of *From Strength To Strength*, Arthur Brooks stated that the seven words you should always remember, which summarize all the lessons in the book are:

Use things

Love people

Worship the divine

You may have issues with the last of the three words if you do not believe in any supernatural being but you should still hold dearly to the first two phrases. You should USE THINGS and LOVE PEOPLE. Sadly, many people USE PEOPLE and LOVE THINGS. The implication of this is that such people only see their relationships with others as an opportunity to gain an advantage.

Words such as loyalty, commitment, and sacrifice do not exist in the dictionary of such people. When such individuals help you, they do it because of something they want to gain from you in the future or immediately. Such people find it easy to break relationships, quit partnerships, and destroy alliances within the blink of an eye. All that matters to them is the monetary gain they will enjoy from any partnership.

Ravi Zacharias, the late Christian apologetic, told a beautiful story that depicts this kind of attitude:

A lady was travelling in an airplane with a stranger. The stranger, a man who appeared to be someone classy, started a conversation with her, "Hello."

"Hi," she responded. Sounding like someone who does not talk much, he asked, "Would you like to have sex with me for one night for a million dollars, after this flight?"

The lady's mouth was ajar with surprise but she quickly gave a response before the seemingly important and serious stranger changed his mind as he was already turning away to continue reading his magazine, "Of course, I will."

The stranger smiled in satisfaction and the lady was proud of herself because she thought she had hit the jackpot by being decisive. She was already thinking about all the nice things she could do with a million dollars when the stranger said something that ended her daydream with a rude shock.

"Will you consider the same offer for ten dollars?" the stranger asked with a mocking smirk on his face.

By now, she was incandescent with rage. With a mixture of annoyance, irritation, frustration, and disappointment, she replied, "What do you take me for? Who do you think I am?"

The stranger turned away from her and started reading his magazine before saying, "We have already decided on that aspect, we are only haggling over the price."

His response implies that the fact that she could agree to sleep with a stranger already makes her a prostitute regardless of the price. Many people are like this. Their so-called values depend on what you offer them. They will continue to be your friend, spouse, or partner as long as no one offers them more money than they can get from you. This is what it means to USE PEOPLE because you LOVE THINGS.

Keeping Your Bridges Intact

When you use people, you will not have respect for the people around you, especially when they are not influential or wealthy. It gets worse with strangers. You might insult Bill Gates on your way to an interview with Microsoft or Mark Zuckerberg on your way to an interview with Facebook when you have low emotional intelligence. Below are some tips that will ensure that do not burn your bridges:

Always Remember That You Need Others

It is rash to think that we do not need anyone. No one has ever been able to succeed all by themselves. In life, you will always need others and that is why you should always treat people well. The gateman you disrespected might be the one that could have saved your life later.

Some people will never forgive you if you hurt them. They will not recommend you when there is an opportunity that you desire. They might even be the ones that will deny you great opportunities in the future. So, you will be shooting yourself in the foot when you treat people unfairly because of their current situation.

Treat Everyone Well

You can never know who you will or will not need. So, it is in your best interest to treat everyone well. You can never tell who will recommend you to someone who will change your life. Over the years, some of the clients that have annoyed me have been the ones that ended up linking me with high-paying clients.

Sometimes I imagine what could have happened if I had treated them badly simply because they frustrated me. Endeavor to be patient with people, especially when they try to get under your skin. You will end up earning their respect when you are patient despite their best effort to annoy you.

End Every Relationship Amicably

When you want to leave your current job role for a new one, it is recommended that you present your resignation letter professionally to your boss. This approach is important because it is an amicable way of ending a professional relationship. You should never end a relationship out of annoyance and frustration because you will always need people.

Even romantic relationships should be handled this way. The fact that you do not want a relationship or marriage anymore does not mean you should subject the person to inhumane treatment. Your ex might become your boss in the future or be in a position to help you later. Do not let the current disappointment make you lose every benefit you could have enjoyed from a person in the future.

Place A Premium On Referral

All my life, I have enjoyed the benefits of having a good relationship with clients and friends. You do not have to beg or hire people to leave good comments on your company's website. If you provide quality service, people will happily refer you to people who need your services and products. According to referral statistics by *Extole*, customers that are gotten via referrals have a 37% chance of staying loyal to the company.

Chapter Two: Self-Criticism

"Remember, you have been criticizing yourself for years and it hasn't worked. Try approving of yourself and see what happens."

Louise Hay

You must be harsh with yourself when you are not performing as expected. You should be objective enough to tell yourself when you are below par to pick yourself up. However, when your poor performance makes you think that you are not good enough, you need to draw the line at that point. Self-criticism is a common self-sabotaging behavior you need to destroy before it makes you stagnant. This chapter will help you with tips that can help you in this regard.

You Are Not That Bad

According to a 2018 study published in *Frontiers in Psychology*, four themes of self-criticism were discovered. They are:

- Feeling ashamed and not wanting to show weakness
- Being harsh or strict with yourself
- Feeling guilty or angry
- Feeling useless or like a burden

Your self-critic always wants you to feel that you are terrible beyond reality. Many times, we feel this way when we compare ourselves with others, especially people who are raves of the moment. We forget that some of these people have also had periods where they did not perform as expected. The truth is that we do not always do the things we should do as human beings.

You should only be concerned if you find yourself repeating the same mistake because that is a sign that you are not learning. It is not a problem to make mistakes because the experience will make you wiser. However, something is wrong when you find yourself repeating the same mistakes all over again. Even the best of us all have low moments. So, the fact that you make mistakes sometimes is perfectly normal because it shows that you are human.

How To Overcome Self-Criticism

Based on the study cited earlier, self-compassion is the most potent weapon against self-criticism. The authors identified six components of self-compassion. They include:

- Guiding your boundaries
- Being gentle with yourself
- Accepting illness and limitations
- Taking responsibility for your health
- Maintaining a positive perspective
- Connecting with others

Guiding Your Boundaries

As mentioned earlier, it is okay to be sincere towards yourself. You should not accept mediocrity. Yet, you should know when you are going overboard. If your daughter has done something wrong, you should correct her but your intention should not be to make her feel worthless. In the same way, you should draw the line when criticizing yourself.

You should not call yourself worthless or useless all because you acted inappropriately. The way you deal with your mistakes determines whether you will recover or give up on yourself. When you call yourself worthless for making a mistake, it might make you struggle to find the motivation to try again. So, you should know where to draw the line.

Being Gentle On Yourself

As a loving father or mother, after correcting your son, you must let him know that you are doing it because you care about him. This will show in your choice of words. You will not resort to name-calling in the process and you will find the next available opportunity to reaffirm your love for him.

This is the same approach you should use when dealing with yourself. It is often easier to forgive others than to forgive ourselves. Yet, you have to be deliberate about being compassionate towards yourself. After rebuking yourself for getting it wrong, remind yourself that you can turn things around. Reaffirm your belief in yourself and your ability to make the best of the situation.

Accepting Illness And Limitations

Sometimes we are critical of ourselves when we contract a terminal disease or fail woefully because we feel it is all our fault. Of course, perhaps you could have handled the situation better, given another chance. Yet, the reality is that you cannot turn back the hands of time. You just have to find a way to make the best of the situation.

No one wants to have to battle cancer or diabetes but these are diseases that many people all over the world suffer from. According to the National Cancer

Institute, approximately 39.5% of men and women in the US will be diagnosed with cancer at some point in their livestimes. The best thing you can do for yourself is to accept the situation and try as much as possible to live your life to the fullest within the limitations of any reality to avoid being excessively critical of yourself.

Taking Responsibility For Your Health

This is critical, especially in a situation where a person is battling a terminal disease. Many people complicate the situation by neglecting their health. Their failure to accept the new reality makes them abhor self-care. Regardless of the nature of the situation, you have to take responsibility for your health.

It could be a divorce, rape, job loss, or the loss of a loved one. Criticizing yourself will not change anything. It will only make your health deteriorate. So, what is best for you to display self-compassion during a chaotic period is to ensure that you take care of yourself.

Maintaining A Positive Perspective

Stressful occurrences such as the death of a loved one, job loss, and divorce can be devastating. Still, they are not the end of the world. There have been many people that have recovered from them to become celebrities. J.K. Rowling, the author of Harry Potter, is a good example in this regard.

She made the best of her divorce to become a superstar. Therefore, you must maintain a positive perspective during a stormy period of your life. It might appear as though all hope is lost but as long as you are alive, there is still hope. Be optimistic and be grateful for the positive things in your life in the meantime.

Connecting With Others

One of the signs of depression is self-isolation. Meanwhile, you can become depressed when you allow your inner critic to get the best of you. It is okay to take your time and spend some time alone to process an unfortunate event. When Cristiano Ronaldo lost his child, he asked for privacy and Bill Gates did the same thing when he divorced his wife. Yet, you should not stay away from your loved ones for too long to avoid making the situation worse.

Chapter Three: Resistance To Change

"Resistance by definition is self-sabotage."

Steven Pressfield

Any individual or organization that is resistant to change will be stagnant. The only constant thing in life is change. If you continue to use second-generation computers in the modern world, you are only shooting yourself in the foot. This chapter will highlight the danger of resisting change and how you can overcome this self-sabotaging attitude.

Changes Are Uncomfortable

In the movie *Madea Homecoming*, Tyler Perry, playing Madea, while speaking to her daughter who had marital issues, spoke some words that should be engraved in marble. He said many people have issues in marriage because they only said "I do" once to one person. Meanwhile, they are meant to say it to different people throughout the marriage.

What she meant by this statement is that people change. The person you agreed to marry will change throughout their life and you have to be ready to love them all over again when they change, to keep the marriage going. Sometimes, the change is positive but sometimes people get worse. We all prefer the devil we know to the one we don't know. Changes are usually uncomfortable because they kick us out of our comfort zone even when they are positive. Yet, we have to prepare and anticipate change because it will happen, whether we like it or not.

Change Is Necessary

Despite how uncomfortable a change can be, changes are necessary for growth and development. It is the changes that occur in the body of a girl that turns her into a woman. In the same way, changes in the body of a boy turn him into a man. As a parent, you will experience the difficult moment when your children will leave home to travel to different places for educational purposes, to places where they will not be under your direct guidance.

At some point, they will leave your home to get married. It is usually a tough transition because you have always been with them. Yet, it is a change you must not resist, to avoid appearing selfish and controlling to your children. In politics, no matter how beautiful and successful the tenure of a leader is, it will come to an end. Others have to take the mantle from the leader and lead the nation or institution.

Dangers Of Resistance To Change

It is recommended that you embrace change and make the best of the situation. If you do not prepare for changes in every area of your life, it has the following consequences:

Stagnancy

Whether personally or car, it is best that you are open to changes because you will be stagnant if you do not move with changing times. Imagine that you choose to keep sending messages through a post office in modern times. You will only be shooting yourself in the foot. As I mentioned earlier, changes are necessary for growth and development.

So, it is not good to always see changes as a threat to you. Indeed, it will be uncomfortable because it might mean that you will have to learn something new. Computer programmers have to learn new programming languages to keep up with innovations. If you want to keep using a method you know when there are better and improved ways of getting more results, you will only stagnate.

Stress

Research has shown that low energy and low productivity are symptoms of resistance to change. These are signs associated with the stress of adapting to a new situation. Your mental health will suffer when you are fighting a lost cause. If a new system was introduced in your workplace, what is best for you is to think of how you can adapt to it.

If you keep complaining about the new system, it will only increase your job stress. In the long run, it will affect your job satisfaction and it might make you seek a new role. If you do not seek a new role, your level of productivity will reduce and you will grumble while working, which will only increase your stress level.

Overstaying Your Welcome

No matter how much people care about you, they will have issues with you when you overstay your welcome. One of the key lessons I learned by reading Arthur Brooks' *From Strength To Strength* is knowing when to quit. Many people do not know to leave when the ovation is loudest.

Resignation is not always the easiest choice but it is an honorable way to leave a position when it is obvious that you no longer have what it takes to continue. The people will respect you for it even when they don't understand your decision. You are at risk of ruining your hard-earned reputation when you continue to stay in a position where you do not possess the qualities that will take the organization or institution to the next level.

Appearing Selfish And Controlling

There is no point in fighting a battle you will never win. For example, as a parent, you cannot expect your children to have the same time and attention after they are married, that they used to have for you before they got married. Your children have started a new phase of life and you have to get used to and respect it.

If you keep demanding their attention as it used to be, you will only appear selfish and controlling. There are times you just have to maintain your distance from people, regardless of how much you love them, to maintain the affection and care. They should consult you when they need your help to maintain your respect.

Depression

When we do not embrace change, we are at risk of isolation. For example, you should prepare for the latter period of your life when you will have to retire. Some people are forced to retire or leave a role they have held for a long time and this makes them depressed.

Their attachment to the role makes it impossible for them to imagine leaving it. The same thing happens to people who lose their spouses due to divorce or death. Indeed, it is usually extremely stressful and painful. Yet, you have to adapt to the new reality to avoid getting depressed.

Chapter Four: Self-Neglect

Based on the discovery of a 2018 study, self-neglect is one of the themes of self-criticism. Meanwhile, self-criticism is self-sabotaging behavior. If you are not willing to take care of yourself, who should? In *12 Rules For Life*, author Jordan Peterson stated that many people care for their pets more than they care for themselves. This chapter will discuss how you can prevent self-neglect to live a happy and fulfilled life.

Causes of Self-Neglect

Despite the selfish tendencies of people, it is surprising to find out that some people display palpable self-neglect. Based on studies, below are some of the causes of self-neglect:

Loss of Loved Ones

According to a 2016 study, the loss of a loved one is one of the major reasons people indulge in self-neglect. The trauma of a sudden event affects people differently. Some people, especially individuals that are resilient and have quality support, usually recover quickly from the occurrence, but this is not the case for others.

Some people take a long time to process the reality and they struggle to eat healthily or exercise their bodies during that time. They will not clean their homes and become vulnerable to diseases. Of course, it hurts and it can be challenging to handle such an occurrence. Yet, the best you can do for yourself is to move on as soon as possible.

Being A Victim Of Violence

This is very common in women, especially the ones in abusive marriages. The trauma of realizing that the man you love is your tormenter and source of sadness is usually difficult to process. Some men would demonstrate so much affection to a woman during courtship only to become monsters after getting married to her. This is one of the reasons some women divorce their husbands.

Of course, there are also rare cases of women emotionally, verbally, and physically abusing their husbands. Either way, this could lead to self-neglect, according to a 2016 study. Indeed, it is usually difficult to cry out because you do not want others to know that your marriage has become hell for you. Yet, it is in your best interest that you seek help as soon as possible instead of resorting to self-neglect while suffering in silence.

Divorce

Most people do not expect to go through a divorce but it is one of the mishaps many people go through in life. It is usually stressful and emotionally demanding, especially when children are involved. It is more challenging to handle when you still want the marriage but the other party has given up on the relationship. You will try to fight for the marriage and the more you do that, the more you will get hurt when the person is not responding.

Mental Illness

According to a 2015 study, mental illnesses, such as depression, is a risk factor for self-neglect. Depression leads to isolation, alcohol, and substance abuse. People battling this issue are at risk of unhealthy eating habits and living a sedentary lifestyle. The impact of their self-neglect shows in their appearance.

Such people lose the motivation to do anything, which makes them lose the desire to cook. They will most likely eat junk and anything they can find, which takes a toll on their health. It gets worse for people battling schizophrenia.

Old Age

According to a 2017 study, many self-neglecting elders are not aware that they are not taking care of themselves. Many of them perceive themselves as "self-care disabled." This is why older people must be supported as much as possible because they tend to act in ways that can jeopardize their health. The fact that they do not have the same strength they had when they were younger to live an independent life, plays a crucial role in this aspect. This is why their children and family members must support them in every possible way.

How To Overcome Self-Neglect

Self-neglect does not have any benefit. It is a self-sabotaging behavior that will deprive you of your physical and mental health. The following tips can help you to overcome it:

Think About The Consequences

One of the ways you can avoid a bad habit is to ruminate on its negative impacts. If the reason you have been neglecting yourself is due to divorce or the loss of a loved one, note that refusing to take care of yourself will not solve the problem. Instead, it will take its toll on your physical and emotional health.

Therefore, you should move on. Of course, it is easier said than done but it is your best and only option. Losing a loved one or going through a divorce is not the end of life. If only you had a glimpse of the beautiful future you could have when you refuse to let it weigh you down, you will summon the courage to move on.

Process The Event

In *The Body Keeps The Score,* author Bessel van der Kolk, M.D., explained that one of the ways you can recover from trauma is by summoning the courage to process the event. You have to do it deliberately to arrive at a conclusion that will help you to move on. When you are scared to do this, you will try to suppress the emotions and flashbacks, which is impossible.

If your mind drives you to the event through a trigger, such as a person saying or acting in ways that remind you of the event, you will be sad all over again. So, it is recommended that you process the event. If it is a divorce, remind yourself of all the efforts you put in to make it work.

Convince yourself that the person does not deserve you. If you can arrive at this kind of conclusion, it will not hurt as much anymore.

Get Support

The way you treat the people around you determines the level of sympathy you will eventually receive. It is not best to pretend that you are strong when you need help. Even when you are resilient, it helps to have people around you that will support you during your stormy days. The encouraging words of your friends and family will go a long way in helping you to recover from an unfortunate event.

Seek Professional Help

The love and support of your loved ones, in tandem with your resilience, should be enough to help you through turbulent times that are making you neglect yourself. However, if it is not working, it is recommended that you seek the help of a therapist to rediscover your self-compassion.

Chapter Five: Procrastination

"If you think of something, do it. Plenty of people often think I'd like to do this or that."

Lydia Davis

It is vital to prepare for the challenges ahead before you start anything. This is essential to avoid a scenario where you quit because you discovered that you are not ready to make the necessary sacrifices that can lead to success in an endeavor. Yet, until you have started, you have not achieved anything. This chapter will explore some useful tips that can help you prevent procrastination.

Why Do People Procrastinate?

The list of self-sabotaging behaviors cannot be complete without mentioning procrastination. Your journey to win your battle over this habit begins with understanding why people procrastinate. Below are some of the reasons people indulge in this habit:

Boredom

You might be wasting time instead of working on a task when you feel it is boring. The boredom might be due to the fact you have been doing the same thing for years. In some cases, it is because there is no one to challenge you. Studies have shown that people have more motivation to do something when others might beat them to it.

Healthy competition always spices up any activity. It is the reason you find yourself driving faster on a busy road than when the road is quiet. Another reason we get bored when carrying out a task is when we do not understand it. Mathematical operations are like that for many people.

Distraction

A distraction is not always negative. Sometimes, it is something legitimate. Yet, the definition of a distraction is anything that prevents you from achieving a goal. For example, there is nothing wrong with watching your favorite football team play in the UEFA Champions League. Nonetheless, if watching the game prevents you from preparing for your presentation in your office the following day, it is a distraction.

Distractions come in various ways. Sometimes, it can even come from the people you love such as your spouse, children, or friends. I once had a friend that talked to me even when I was trying to complete a manuscript. I know that he loves me and enjoys being around me, yet, I had to let him know that I would not be able to focus on work if he kept talking to me. So, we had to strike a balance between when to talk and when he should let me work.

Lack Of Skills

When you lack the skills required to carry out a task, you will not be motivated to work on it. For example, if you are a student that is deficient in research work, writing your dissertation will feel like you are being told to climb Mount Kilimanjaro. However, for people who know what to do, it is straightforward.

Low Motivation

There are various reasons we lack the motivation to work on a task. Sometimes, it might be since the monetary gain is small. It might also be due to the lack of appreciation shown in the past towards you, after completing such a task for the same person. For example, if your spouse is critical of you whenever you help him or her with a house chore, you might be discouraged to help out the next time. You might waste time thinking about whether the effort is worth it or not before starting.

How To Overcome Procrastination

Procrastination is not an incurable disease. It is a bad habit that will make you achieve little. Below are some proven tips that can help you avoid wasting time:

Negotiate

If the reason you are struggling to start a task is that you are not happy with the financial reward package, you should negotiate your pay rather than waste time.

You do not have to undertake a task when you are not happy to do it. It is not true that you will not find a better offer. If you are certain that you deserve better, negotiate the pay. The person may be willing to offer you more money as long as you guarantee to do a good job. You'll never know until you ask.

Acquire Skills

There is no point in deceiving yourself. If you lack the skills required to carry out a task, admit it and let the person know that you cannot do it. Alternatively, if you have time to acquire the skills required, pend the job and learn how to go about it first. It usually appears as though you are performing magic when you are efficient at doing something. On the other hand, you will struggle when you do not know what to do. You will only end up wasting precious time.

Cut Out Potential Distractions

As mentioned earlier, your distractions are usually things that appeal to you but they will prevent you from achieving your goals. You must identify your potential distractions so that you can avoid them. For example, if you work from home, it might be difficult to separate work from family affairs. You might have to use somewhere outside your home as office space so that you can concentrate solely on the work whenever you are working.

Seek Clarity

Sometimes, you do not need to acquire special skills to carry out a task. You might only need to ask the right questions from the right people to get useful answers. The vastness of the internet can come in handy in this regard. However, sometimes, you might need to find people in your field or sphere of influence that has the answers to your question. Talk to them to get clarity and avoid wasting time.

Spice It Up

Finding a way to spice up a task might be all that you need to do it faster. For example, you might introduce music when carrying out house chores. It can also help with exercise. Nonetheless, you mustn't allow what ought to be a spice to become a source of distraction.

Chapter Six: Perfectionism

"If you look for perfection, you will never be content."

Leo Tolstoy

Success addiction cannot be separated from perfectionism. It is what makes you want more and more until the wheels come off. It is the reason many people struggle to enjoy their success. It is the same reason some people feel empty despite their remarkable achievements. This chapter will discuss what makes perfectionism a self-sabotaging behavior and how you can overcome it.

Signs Of Perfectionism

Perfectionists usually struggle to admit it. They feel that they are only trying to be excellence-oriented. There is nothing wrong with wanting to do things in the best possible way. However, it is a problem when you always want things to be perfect. According to Walden University, you can tell that you have a perfectionist tendency when you discover these signs:

You Want Every Area Of Your Life To Be Perfect

There is nothing wrong with demanding the best from yourself in an area of your life such as your career. However, it is a problem when this tendency shows in every area of your life. Perfectionists will be angry if their kids move a piece of furniture some centimeters away from where they left it. They will berate their spouse for overcooking the pasta.

Always Angry With Being Second

It is fine that you believe you have the capacity to lead but you cannot always be the leader. There are times when you will have to be patient until the opportunity arises to lead. However, perfectionists will always find fault with their leaders because they believe that they can do better if given the opportunity. Meanwhile, the fact that you can excel in a role does not mean you should frustrate the efforts of the person currently occupying that role.

People's Approval Mean A Lot To You

One of the reasons perfectionists try to be perfect in everything they do is that they seek the approval of others. They are always trying to impress someone. They want visitors to find their homes in perfect condition so that they can believe they are neat. They want their hair to look perfect so that the opposite sex will be attracted to them.

You Are Usually Defensive

Due to their insatiable desire to look perfect, perfectionists are usually defensive when confronted with their flaws. They do not want anyone to think that they can do anything wrong. So, to avoid appearing vulnerable, they prefer to make excuses for their errors. Consequently, they never apologize, frustrating the people around them.

You Always Find Fault With Others

Perfectionists never praise the effort of others. They will also find a reason to underplay the achievement of others because they do not want others to take the center stage instead of them. When they are your leaders, they will frustrate you in the guise of challenging you to try harder.

You Procrastinate A Lot

In their bid to produce something perfect, perfectionists usually waste a lot of time. They do not want anyone to be able to criticize them because they are always critical of others. So, they hardly start anything until they are very sure it will come out perfectly.

You Struggle To Forgive Yourself And Others

Due to the unrealistic demands on themselves and others, perfectionists are hard to please. When people around them do not meet their standards, they are quick to wield the axe. When they are the ones that are found wanting, they struggle to forgive themselves, especially when others find out about their failure.

How To Overcome Perfectionism

Perfectionism can lead to health issues such as stress, exhaustion, anxiety, suicidal thoughts, eating disorders, frustration, and obsessive-compulsive disorder. It can also destroy your professional and interpersonal relationships. You can win the battle against perfectionistic tendencies by leveraging the following tips:

Realize It Is A Problem

Until you believe that something is a problem, you will not make deliberate efforts to solve it. So, you must discover the disadvantages of being a perfectionist so that you can work on them. At some point in my life, I had this tendency because I demanded a lot from myself. However, I am grateful that a colleague pointed it out. He helped me realize that I was always trying to outdo others. This made it difficult for me to celebrate with others because I was always feeling like they were taking my place.

I have not stopped placing high demands on myself but I am no longer afraid to fail. Also, I no longer have issues with celebrating others. I still have a strong excellence mindset but I am no longer too critical of myself. Whenever I fail, I pick myself up, assuring myself that I will do better next time. This approach has also helped me to be less critical of others. Before now, some of my friends avoided speaking around me because I would be quick to point out their errors, interrupting them instead of listening to them, which strained my relationship with them.

Deal With The Source

Some of the reasons people have perfectionistic tendencies include:

- Striving for approval
- Fear of failure
- Previous success
- Success addiction

Your desire to be perfect might not be due to all of the factors listed above but it is usually due to one or more of them. It is recommended that you take your time to discover the cause of this issue, to deal with it. If the fear of failure is the problem, then you need to let yourself know that it is okay to fail sometimes. You must lift this pressure from your shoulders so that you can strive for success without trying to be perfect.

Seek A Professional

You might need the help of a therapist to solve perfectionism problems, especially when they are deep-rooted. Usually, a therapist will use either hypnotherapy, cognitive-behavior therapy, or family systems therapy to help you. Cognitive-behavior therapy involves helping you to understand that you do not have to be perfect in every area of your life.

Hypnotherapy is used to eliminate the "all or nothing" mindset, which is a problem many perfectionists have. Meanwhile, family systems therapy tries to discover the role of your family background in turning you into a perfectionist. Some people are never comfortable with second place because of the high demands their parents placed on them when they were young.

Chapter Seven: Impatience

If you achieve anything in a hurry, the chances are high that it will leave you with scars. Impatience is a self-sabotaging behavior that makes people wish they waited before acting rashly. Of course, patience is one of the most challenging virtues to possess in a jet speed world. Yet, it is very critical to living a happy and meaningful life. This chapter will discuss the dangers of impatience and how you can overcome this habit.

Symptoms Of Impatience

The reality is that being patient is easier said than done. Yet, you need it to avoid making hasty decisions that can have grave consequences. You can know if you are impatient when you see these signs:

Desperation

Whenever you are desperate, you are at risk of making a decision that will backfire. Desperation makes you unable to see the dangers ahead. Instead, all that you will be concerned about is the benefit you stand to enjoy from the decision. When you make an investment decision on this basis, you will only focus on the opportunities, convincing yourself that you are a risk-taker.

Indeed, you have to take risks to stand the chance of success in this world. Yet, it has to be calculated risks that have low chances of going haywire. However, when you are desperate, the fact that the risk is excessive will matter little to you and this is the reason people get defrauded.

Anxiety

Anxiety makes you worry about something that might never happen. Studies have shown that anxiety over finance is the number one source of anxiety among American adults. When you are worried, it is a sign that you do not have concrete plans about your future or you are impatient. A plan does not automatically mean that you will succeed. Yet, when you have a concrete plan that you trust, the chances of being anxious are limited.

Inability To Enjoy The Moment

Impatient people struggle to enjoy their current level. Instead of making the best of their time in college, they are already looking forward to when they will start earning money, disrupting their commitment and performance in school. In the same way, some people find it difficult to enjoy their days of being single. They just want to be in a relationship at all costs.

Of course, the fact that you are patient does not mean inactivity. It is being deliberate about the next phase in such a way that you can enjoy the current level. Train yourself to enjoy every stage and moment of your life. This approach will give you the platform to make informed and deliberate decisions about your future.

A Pattern Of Hasty Decisions

Nothing shows you are impatient more than hasty decisions. One of the ways you can know that you are fond of making hasty decisions is instability. You will find yourself starting and stopping many things. Such a person will start a business and quit to start a new one. At some point, such a person will decide he wants to be an entrepreneur only to pick up a job not long after that.

Prioritizing Instant Gratification

Instant gratification implies preferring short-term benefits to long-term advantages. This is the hallmark of impatience. An impatient person will ignore the long-term benefits and consequences of his or her action as long as there is something to enjoy immediately. This approach inhibits sustainable and substantial growth and development.

How To Overcome Impatience

You can deliberately work on your patience level. The following tips will help you in this regard:

Employ Consequential Thinking

Consequential thinking is an approach that makes you consider the short and long-term consequences of your action before acting. Many people lack this approach to life, which makes them make rash decisions that they will regret or have to apologize for later. When people often ask you "what were you thinking?" when you do things, it is a sign that you need to up your consequential thinking game.

When you have a good grasp of the consequences of your actions, it will help you to avoid the ones that can affect you negatively in the future, effectively eradicating impatience. Speaking impulsively is also a form of impatience. So, employ consequential thinking even before you speak.

Draw Examples From Other People's Experiences

You do not have to experience everything yourself in life. Experience might be a good teacher but it usually teaches nasty lessons. Therefore, it is not recommended to always learn by experience. You would have wasted a lot of time before you knew what to do. Instead, learn from the experiences of others.

For example, you do not have to invest in a Ponzi scheme and lose your money before you understand that such an approach to making money is not worth it. It is a get-rich-quick approach that is built on impatience and greed. By learning from others who have made a mistake by being impatient, you can avoid the same mistakes.

Do Not Overrate Your Own Opinion

One of the reasons people make hasty decisions is that they overrate their own opinions. Of course, you should trust your decisions, especially when they are informed and objective. However, considering the opinion of others gives you another point of view that will enable you to test the quality of your decisions. So, one of the ways you can detect impatience in your decisions is by listening to the people you trust.

Avoid Trends

In the earlier part of this book, we discussed the danger of being resistant to change. We explained that this approach will hinder your productivity. Yet, it is not every trend you need to follow. For example, you cannot jump on every fashion trend. This approach will only make you buy clothes that you will not want to wear in the long run.

Also, the fact that people are investing in cryptocurrency does not mean you have to do the same. You cannot invest in every business idea that appears.

Like an opportunity to earn money. It is better to stick with a business model that offers you a steady income than to take risks that will lead to bankruptcy.

Avoid Instant Gratification

You have mastered the art of patience when you can overcome the temptation of choosing instant gratification over long-term benefits. This is the reason you will choose to support the current leader even when you have better qualities. When you become the leader, you will have less opposition when you have been loyal to your previous leaders.

When you do the right thing at the wrong time, you are only setting yourself up. When you are patient, you will wait for the right time to pounce. Every opportunity is not what it appears to be. Some opportunities are traps that can truncate your future. So, look before you leap. Your appetite and desires should not be the reason you make decisions. Think about the long-term benefits and disadvantages.

Chapter Eight: Self-Objectification

One of the battles superstars face all through their careers and lives is self-objectification. Some people struggle to see you beyond a certain aspect of your life. For example, all that many people saw about Michael Jackson were his performances as a pop star. Meanwhile, he was more than a pop star. He was a human being who had family and personal issues. However, he was objectified. Sadly, sometimes we objectify ourselves to shoot ourselves in the foot. This chapter will focus on this and how you can avoid it.

You Are More Than Your Job

In *Identity*, rapper Lecrae Moore said: *"I'm not the shoes I wear*

I'm not the clothes I buy
I'm not the house I live in
I'm not the car I drive, no"

You can include "I'm not my job" in the list. We live in a world where the opinion of others about us matters too much to many people. Thankfully, some people understand that awards are usually based on sentiments. The acceptance speech of Drake during the 2019 Grammy, remains iconic in this regard. He said:

"I want to take this opportunity while I'm up here to just talk to all the kids that are watching this, aspiring to do music," Drake said. "All my peers that make music from their heart that do things pure and tell the truth, I wanna let you know we're playing in an opinion-based sport, not a factual-based sport. So it's not the NBA where at the end of the year you're holding a trophy because you

made the right decisions or won the games."

He added:

"This is a business where sometimes it's up to a bunch of people who might not understand what a mixed-race kid from Canada has to say or a fly Spanish girl from New York or anybody else, or a brother from Houston right there, my brother Travis [Scott]. But my point is you've already won if you have people singing your songs word for word if you're a hero in your hometown. Look, if there are people who have regular jobs who are coming out in the rain, in the snow, spending their hard-earned money to buy tickets to come to your shows, you don't need this right here. I promise you, you already won."

It must have been shocking for the organizers of the award. The broadcast cut to commercial before he finished speaking but it was too late. He had made his point.

Many people might have issues with him but he has told the truth many people cannot speak and do not want to hear. We are not defined by our jobs and awards.

Avoid The Temptation

As a celebrity, people will always want to objectify you. Sometimes, they defend you when they should not and it gets so bad that some people mock competitors regarding sensitive issues in their lives. For example, when Cristiano Ronaldo lost his son, some of the fans of his eternal rival, Lionel Messi, were mocking him. This is ridiculous. Yet, this is how far people will go to idolize and objectify people.

It gets worse when you are the one thinking you are impeccable and untouchable simply because of the great achievements you have in your career. Do not let your money and achievement go to your head. People may sing your praises to the high heavens but you have to stay grounded. If you allow the desire to stay at the top of your game to ruin your interpersonal relationships, you will regret it eventually.

How To Overcome Self-Objectification

Self-objectification puts you at risk of disregarding other important areas of your life. It can also make you desperate to maintain your success at any cost, which can ruin you. You can avoid this self-sabotaging behavior by leveraging the tips below:

Always Remember That You Are Human

As a celebrity, your fans will always want you to forget that you are a human being. They will always want more and more regardless of what is happening to them. The late Michael Jackson was going through a lot but many people were either ignorant of his troubles or did not care. All that mattered to them was for him to entertain them. He was nothing but a toy that could amuse them with his fancy dancing steps and melodic voice.

His sufferings became real to many people after his death and many of them began to buy his recordings after his death. People will move on, while you lose yourself or your life living to please them. So, always remind yourself that you are a human being, especially at the height of your stardom.

Remember What Matters

Whatever will matter eventually, should matter to you now. It is not best to sacrifice your health and interpersonal relationships to achieve career success.

You will retire eventually unless you are a monarch. Therefore, do not let the addiction to the limelight make you abandon your family and friends. If anything should happen to you, you will not see your fans. It is your loved ones that will be there for you.

Have An Exit Plan

Your body will not be able to go on and on indefinitely. If you are an athlete, you will have to stop at some point and the same goes for anyone involved in any career that is energy-intensive. Even when your job does not demand a lot of energy, you will have to stop at some point. It is risky when you let your body stop you because it might mean you will be battling a terminal disease by then. So, have an exit plan that will make it possible to enjoy your health for a reasonable period, for the rest of your life.

Stay Sensitive And Empathetic

Some celebrities are fond of throwing shades at themselves and their fans pick up the bitterness. Sadly, some people do not know where to draw the line. Showing kindness and empathy is not a sign of weakness. When Cristiano Ronaldo lost his son, Liverpool Football Club sent their condolences despite their rivalry with Manchester United. That is a good gesture that should be applauded.

Chapter Nine: Distrust

Motivational speakers and life coaches will encourage you to trust no one. Well, it is dangerous to rely on people, especially when they have not proven that they deserve it. Yet, you cannot show distrust towards everyone around you because it hurts, especially when you act that way towards the people that genuinely care for you. This chapter will discuss the causes of distrust and how you can handle it.

The Dangers Of Extreme Lack Of Trust

Showing an extreme lack of trust is unhealthy and it has several consequences. Here are some of them:

Insecurity

When you struggle to trust anyone, you will always feel like you are in danger. You will always be acting toward people as though everyone around you has plans to hurt you. This insecurity will also affect the way you treat people that bring opportunities your way. You will act suspiciously towards them as though they are only looking for an opportunity to take advantage of you. There is nothing wrong with being careful but it is not right to assume that everyone that comes near you is trying to hurt you.

Anxiety

Distrust will make you scared even when there is no reason... It gets so bad for some people that they think every government policy is based on an ulterior motive to hurt them. Meanwhile, anxiety can affect your blood pressure, which can lead to hypertension and other heart diseases. As mentioned earlier, there is nothing wrong with being careful. You should double-check anything before committing to it. Still, extreme distrust will make you bear a burden that should not be yours.

Low Emotional Intelligence

Anxiety and other emotional problems associated with distrust, make an individual have low emotional intelligence. You will struggle to handle stress and other uncomfortable situations because you will usually be on the verge of freaking out. This state of mind puts you at risk of unprecedented outbursts and rage that you will realize was never worth it.

Relationship Issues

It will be evident to the people around you that you do not trust them and it is hurtful.

No one wants to hang around people that do not trust them. When former Chelsea player, Tammy Abraham was asked why he flourished in AS Roma but struggled towards the last part of his Chelsea career, his answer was succinct – trust.

He simply needed a manager that would show faith in his ability. We all want to be trusted and that is why we should not make others feel we do not trust them, especially when they have not given us any reason to doubt them. If you act this way towards your loved ones, you will struggle to have quality relationships with them.

Why People Struggle To Trust Others

Some people stopped trusting others for specific reasons. Here are some of them:

Previous Experiences

You should learn from your previous experiences. It is a sign of intelligence. The reason some people struggle to trust others is that they have trusted someone in the past who hurt them. For example, some women have trusted men in their previous relationships who used the secrets they shared against them. It would be difficult for such women to trust men again. They are afraid of getting hurt again and the carryover effect of the hurt shows in their subsequent relationships.

Movies And Media

What you watch and read matters. If you have seen too many horror movies where a psychopath was lurking around killing people, it might be difficult for you to move around without such scenes replaying in your mind. If you always see too many movies and stories in the media about heartbreaks, the chances are high that you will struggle to trust anyone with your heart. Every partner will begin to appear like a potential heartbreaker to you.

Family Upbringing

The kind of home you grew up in plays a vital role in determining many aspects of your life. If you grow up in an abusive home, it likely affects your perception of people. For example, if you are a lady who watched your father emotionally and physically abuse your mother, you likely want to prevent a repeat of that at all costs, which might make you have trust issues with men.

How To Defeat Distrust

There are various reasons people struggle to trust others. Yet, you have more to gain by showing faith in others. You can defeat this tendency by taking advantage of the following tips.

Understand Its Consequences

We started this chapter by listing the consequences of extreme distrust. Leverage this information to understand that this habit has self-sabotaging potential. You do not want to have strained relationships with your friends, spouse, children, and colleagues. Besides, the mental health damage it can cause you should make you seek an alternative. This alternative will make you more vulnerable but you need it to live a happy and fulfilled life.

Feed On The Right Things

Some movies portray romantic relationships as something that makes you vulnerable. Such movies are full of quotes such as "love makes you weak." In the same way, some movies portray romantic relationships as something beautiful and worthwhile. It is recommended that you are picky about the things you give your attention to. You are a product of the things you read, hear, and see. So, you must be deliberate in this regard.

Start Small

It is not healthy to show extreme distrust towards others. Nonetheless, it is also not prudent to dive straight in whenever you meet people. Trust should be earned. Therefore, start small, especially if you have had previous negative experiences with trusting people. Give people the chance to win you over, rather than assume that they will hurt you when you let them.

Have A Close Circle Of Friends

As you grow older, what you will realize is that you do not need the crowd. Rather, all that you need is a close circle of trusted friends and associates. This will reduce your chances of getting hurt. Your close circle of friends has been tested and trusted over time, giving you reasons to be vulnerable to them without fear.

Subscribe To Reason Instead Of Emotions

Emotions are deceptive and this is why you should subscribe to the voice of reason when it comes to trust. Make your research about a company or individual before trusting them with your money. In the same way, ask questions from the people that know a person and pay attention to how he or she treats others before deciding to spend the rest of your life with them.

Conclusion

This is such a beautiful journey I do not want to end. A part of me feels like making this a series that will have another sequel. At the time of researching materials that are relevant to this book, I was overwhelmed by what I found. I had to somehow squeeze so much into this short book.

There is no doubt that this guide is a summary of the effort and hard work of various men and women who desire to give others a better life. Some of them did not even get to experience the happiness they desire to give you. Many of them made mistakes that they do not want others to make.

This journey has dealt with how you can treat people right to avoid blocking your path in life. We also discussed procrastination, self-objectification, impatience, self-neglect, self-criticism, perfectionism, resistance to change, and distrust. I am convinced that you learned one or two things from each chapter. You have been equipped with the information you need to live a successful life free of self-sabotage. Go champ!

References

Alizadeh, S., Khanahmadi, S., Vedadhir, A., and Barjasteh, S. (2018). The relationship between resilience with self-compassion social support and sense of belonging in women with breast cancer. *Asian Pacific. J. Cancer Prevent.* 19, 2469–2474. DOI: 10.22034/APJCP.2018.19.9.2469

Callebaut, L., Molyneux, P., and Alexander, T. (2017). The Relationship Between Self-Blame for the Onset of a Chronic Physical Health Condition and Emotional Distress: a Systematic Literature Review. *Clin. Psychol. Psychother.* 24, 965–986. doi: 10.1002/cpp.2061

Duskin, C. (2017, July 31). *15 Referral Marketing Statistics You Need to Know | Extole.* Extole | Referral

Marketing Platform. https://www.extole.com/blog/15-referral-marketing-statistics-you-need-to-know/

Finra. (2021b, April 28). *Large Number of Americans Reported Financial Anxiety and Stress Even Before the Pandemic | FINRA.org.* https://www.finra.org/media-center/newsreleases/2021/large-number-americans-reported-financial-anxiety-and-stress-even

Howard-Jones, P. & Jay, T. (2016). Reward, learning and games. *Current Opinion in Behavioral Sciences, 10*, 65-72.

Hulsbergen, M., and Bohlmeijer, E. T. (2015). *Compassie Als Sleutel Tot Geluk; Voorbij Stress En Zelfkritiek.* Netherlands: Uitgeverij Boom.

National Institute of Cancer. *Cancer of Any Site - Cancer Stat Facts. SEER.*

https://seer.cancer.gov/statfacts/html/all.html

Neff, K. (2016). The Self-Compassion Scale is a Valid and Theoretically Coherent Measure of Self-Compassion. *Mindfulness 7*, 264–274. doi: 10.1007/s12671-015-0479-3

Pew Research. (2021, September 28). *3. How Americans view their jobs.* Pew Research Center's Social & Demographic Trends Project. Retrieved March 12, 2022, from https://www.pewresearch.org/social-trends/2016/10/06/3-how-americans-view-their-jobs/

Rehman, N. (2021). *The Psychology of Resistance to Change: The Antidotal Effect of Organizational Justice, Support and Leader-Member Exchange.* Frontiers. https://www.frontiersin.org/articles/10.3389/fpsyg.2021.678952/full

Walden University. (2022, January 26). *7 Signs You're Too Much of a Perfectionist*. Psychology Careers | Walden University. https://www.waldenu.edu/online-masters-programs/ms-in-psychology/resource/seven-signs-you-are-too-much-of-a-perfectionist

Wilkinson & Finkbeiner, LLP. (2022, March 3). *Divorce Statistics and Facts | What Affects Divorce Rates in the U.S.?* Retrieved March 12, 2022, from https://www.wf-lawyers.com/divorce-statistics-and-facts/

Thank you for reading this book!

If you found this book helpful, I would be grateful if you would **post an honest review on Amazon** so this book can reach other supportive readers like you!

All you need to do is digitally flip to the back and leave your review. Or visit amazon.com/author/senseipauldavid click the correct book cover and click on the blue link next to the yellow stars that say, "customer reviews."

As always...
It's a great day to be alive!

Get/Share Our FREE All-Ages Mental Health Book Now!

FREE Self-Development Book for Every Family

senseiselfdevelopment.senseipublishing.com

Click Below or Search Amazon for Another Book In This Series Or Visit:

www.amazon.com/author/senseipauldavid

www.senseipublishing.com

@senseipublishing
#senseipublishing

Check out our **recommendations** for other books for adults & kids plus other great resources by visiting www.senseipublishing.com/resources/

Join Our Publishing Journey!

If you would like to receive FREE BOOKS and special offers, please visit www.senseipublishing.com and join our newsletter by entering your email address in the pop-up box

Follow Our Engaging Blog NOW! senseipauldavid.ca

Get Our FREE Books Today!

Click & Share the Link Below

FREE Self-Development Book
senseiselfdevelopment.senseipublishing.com

**FREE BONUS!!!
Experience Over 25 FREE Engaging Guided Meditations!**

Prized Skills & Practices for Adults & Kids. Help Restore Deep Sleep, Lower Stress, Improve Posture, Navigate Uncertainty & More.

Download the Free Insight Timer App and click the link below:
http://insig.ht/sensei_paul

About Sensei Publishing

Sensei Publishing commits itself to help people of all ages transform into better versions of themselves by providing high-quality and research-based self-development books with an emphasis on mental health and guided meditations. Sensei Publishing offers well-written e-books, audiobooks, paperbacks and online courses that simplify complicated but practical topics in line with its mission to inspire people towards positive transformation.

It's a great day to be alive!

About the Author

I create simple & transformative eBooks & Guided Meditations for Adults & Children proven to help navigate uncertainty, solve niche problems & bring families closer together.

I'm a former finance project manager, private pilot, jiu-jitsu instructor, musician & former University of Toronto Fitness Trainer. I prefer a science-based approach to focus on these & other areas in my life to stay humble & hungry to evolve. I hope you enjoy my work and I'd love to hear your feedback.

- It's a great day to be alive!
Sensei Paul David

Scan & Follow/Like/Subscribe: Facebook, Instagram, YouTube: @senseipublishing

Scan using your phone/iPad camera for Social Media Visit us at www.senseipublishing.com and sign up for our newsletter to learn more about our exciting books and to experience our FREE Guided Meditations for Kids & Adults.

www.ingramcontent.com/pod-product-compliance
Lightning Source LLC
Chambersburg PA
CBHW071113030426
42336CB00013BA/2058